The Treasure of
Staying
Connected
for Military Couples

Janel Lange

ser&iam
PUBLISHING

Kingsport, Tennessee

www.serviampublishing.com

The Treasure of **Staying Connected**
for Military Couples

©2004 by Janel Lange

ISBN: 0-9754986-0-6

2nd Printing, October 2008

Cover design by deWit designs
www.dewitdesigns.com
Kingsport, Tennessee

Layout by Rainbow Graphics
Kingsport, Tennessee

Printed by United Book Press, Inc., Baltimore, Maryland

Library of Congress Control Number: 2004094808

For information:

SERVIAM PUBLISHING
POST OFFICE BOX 3467
KINGSPORT, TENNESSEE 37664-0467
www.serviampublishing.com

Contents

Acknowledgments v

Introduction vii

Chapter One: Beginning 1

Chapter Two: Awakening 9

Chapter Three: Strengthening 17

Chapter Four: Savoring 31

Chapter Five: Lyn's Story 39

Chapter Six: Chris' Story 47

Chapter Seven: Jaye's Story 59

Chapter Eight: Bob's Story 69

Conclusion 75

Resources for Staying Connected . . . 79

This book is dedicated to all those military men and women who did not return home, and to their families.

Acknowledgments

Many people whom I have met along life's journey have become the model for this little book. Most of what I share in these pages I have unwittingly gleaned from them over the years. I have learned from their example of living grace-filled lives of intimacy with others. I give thanks for all of those people.

As I look back on the development of this book, there are particular persons to whom I am especially grateful:

—Robert Allen and Mark Victor Hansen for their inspiration and encouragement

—My dear friends, Ginger Mayer and Marie O'Neil, both seasoned English teachers, who so gently guided me through editing

—Ann Vachon, whose art is so filled with grace, for capturing the heart of my message in the image on the front cover, and Mary DeWit, who caught the vision and refined it

—Bishop Jack Kaising, who has once again demonstrated his dedication to married couples by the attention he has given to this project

—Nick and Dianne Monje, for their enthusiastic encouragement.

—The professionals at Rainbow Graphics and United Book Press who guided me through this publication with kindness and patience

— My loving husband, Bob, without whom I would not have the life experience to write this book, for all his affirmation and behind the scenes assistance, and yielding the computer time to me!

Introduction

A number of years ago, dear friends sent us a card whose cover read, "Rich is not how much you have, or where you are going, or even what you are. Rich is who you have beside you.— JIK.II" It spoke to me so compellingly that I placed it in an elegant frame, and it hangs on our entryway wall. I pass it many times a day. I can't tell you that I notice it every time I pass by, but when I do, it is a wonderful reminder to me of how rich I truly am. On my life's journey, I have amassed a treasure chest brimming with people who have enriched me in numerous ways. The largest, most brilliant gem in my treasure chest is the man with whom I have made a home for the past thirty-four years. Certainly, on the day that we established our marriage covenant, neither of us could have imagined the rich journey in store for us! Our riches have not been the general garden variety that the world regards as great wealth. Our ever-growing abundance has been an ongoing unfolding of our knowledge and understanding of each other, and of God's graceful presence within our marriage from the beginning, even when we were not aware of it. This is not to say that life has been just a bowl of cherries. We have been an ordinary couple with the ordinary trials of life. But God placed some other ordinary people on the path with us who have been extraordinary examples to us of how to live together with the understanding that our marriage was never intended by God to be just for our own benefit but also for the world in which we live.

Over time, we have come to understand that we are compelled to share our treasure with others. At a conference I attended, I heard bestselling authors Robert Allen and Mark Victor Hansen say that each of us has a book inside of us and that each of us has some area of expertise that could benefit others. My mental wheels started to turn. I had never seriously considered writing a book before. It soon came to me that my years of working in marriage enrichment programs, combined with my years of experience as a military spouse, have given me a perspective that could benefit others. The realization has become an urgency for me! I could have written this book much earlier, and I wish that I had thought of it sooner. I think of couples who want to keep their marriages a priority despite the demands of living a military lifestyle. Sometimes it is difficult to know how to accomplish that.

Perhaps some of the·ideas I share in this book will help. I invite you to take what you can use, and keep your marriage as your greatest treasure. Hopefully, the two of you will be together long after you or your spouse has left active duty, and these little ways of keeping that treasure gleaming will continue to work for you. You can find the resources I mention in the text of the book listed in the back for easy access. You will also find some stories about other military couples—some of those gems in my life whom I mentioned earlier—that may give you more ideas about how to keep your special marriage bond as strong as it can be. God bless you as the two of you serve our country!

CHAPTER ONE

Beginning

As a teenager, I made a sound resolution never to marry a man who went to sea. I grew up in the seaport of New Orleans, and my dad made his living in the merchant marine. He was at sea when I was born and was away for most of the years when my sister and I were growing up. His vacation periods often lasted four to six weeks, when we took family trips by train or car. What I remember most fondly about vacation time were summer days when we hung out together, listening to or watching major league baseball games, as my dad passed on his love of the sport to us. The remainder of his time with us consisted of periods of a week or so between voyages that lasted months. It was exciting for each of us to receive many letters and occasional calls from far away places. The communications technology at that time was infinitesimal compared with that of today, so phone calls were a rare treat. Although we were always confident of his love for us, our family missed my dad's physical presence with us. As the only merchant marine family in the neighborhood, we had wonderful neighbors, but our family nonetheless experienced a sense of isolation. We were the only kids whose dad was not usually around, and my mom was the only wife left to manage the household on her own. Understandably, since the people around us did not have the experience of family separation, they could not fully comprehend the loss our family experienced. In fact, we ourselves did not fully identify the loss objectively.

We were just living life as it presented itself to us.

When Bob, my high school sweetheart, returned from a tour of active duty, he became a reservist, and we married soon afterward. I was confident we would live happily ever after in our hometown. I delighted in having someone around who enjoyed taking care of me. Nine years later, with two young children, I surprised myself as I determined with my husband that he would return to active duty, and we would become a Navy family. We were off on an adventure, and Charleston, SC was our first home away from home. Another Navy family in our new neighborhood quickly embraced us. They had experienced a similar entry into this new lifestyle, and seemed to anticipate our questions before they occurred to us. We were impressed by the support we received, and soon realized we had found a new family, which included a gracious chapel community at the nearby Charleston Air Force base. In the first few months in our new home, our new life was unfolding better than I could have imagined.

After a couple of months, it was time for Bob to head for Newport, R. I., for several months of Navy schooling. The day of his departure, he decided to wait for our first grader to come home from school so he could have a proper farewell with her. After a few hugs, he was on his way. As her dad drove off, our daughter complained to me that her belly itched, and we spent the next three weeks dealing with chicken pox, first hers, then her little brother's! I was christened as a Navy wife.

If you are a military spouse, I suspect that reading this strikes a familiar chord!

It is likely that you, too, have been faced with an unexpected situation which you were forced to deal with on your own. Murphy's Law seems to insure it. I hope that when each situation was resolved, you felt the same sense of accomplishment that I did. Certainly, a valuable lesson most military spouses learn is the magnitude of their own capabilities. Many wives I have met over the years have exuded confidence after the experience of repeated military separations. Some of them have maintained loving marriages despite the trials of months of separation, and readjust fairly easily when reunited with their spouses. Others have expressed difficulty in having their household routines disrupted by the return of their spouses. Other dynamics that I have seen are more subtle. Although the marriage relationship remains benign on the surface, there is a degree of emotional detachment that can occur during a deployment. This can be a sort of defense mechanism to deal with the pain of separation. Fortunately, many marriages survive this process, but some of the emotional intimacy of the marriage can be sacrificed along the way. Gradually, the relationship can become increasingly one of tolerance. I have seen wives who immerse themselves in doing their own thing, while their husbands immerse themselves in their careers.

Fostering an ongoing growth in qualities of unity, intimacy, harmony, and joyfulness in a marriage relationship can be an increased challenge to a military couple. In a society that holds a diminishing value on marriage, with a 50% divorce rate, military marriages are further stressed by the demands of a lifestyle that requires commitment beyond the call of duty. Most couples, whether civilian or military, marry because they want to share their lives together. Somehow, along the way, the busyness of life can get in the way of the sharing part, and we wind up sacrificing, to some degree, the emotional intimacy that energized us in courtship and the early days of marriage. Additionally for military couples, the demands of frequent moves and frequent separations can further stress marital relationships. It takes special attention from both partners to withstand all that tugs and pulls spouses in different directions. Often these tugs and pulls evolve so insidiously that many couples are not fully aware of the resulting stress on their relationships until it reaches a crisis level. Even when they see it coming, couples can find themselves at a loss about how to keep from becoming sucked into the busy life that can become a wedge between loving partners. It requires conscious effort for a couple to maintain the closeness that they treasure when the marriage is new.

CHAPTER TWO

Awakening

When Bob returned from his Navy schools, he was assigned to a ship that was undergoing a shipyard overhaul. Although his work hours were very long, he was able to come home most nights. The time we had as a family was something we really cherished. One Sunday, a couple came to the Air Force chapel and spoke to our congregation about Marriage Encounter. We remembered good friends back home who had invited us to experience a Marriage Encounter weekend several years previously, when we both worked a lot on weekends. We had never found the time to accept their invitations. But now, after months of separation, it seemed like a good idea. Another Navy couple in the neighborhood expressed an interest in experiencing Marriage Encounter as well, so we made an agreement to trade childcare. So, off we went to be alone together for an entire weekend!

What was so remarkable about this get-away weekend was that it would continue to positively impact the quality of our relationship for the rest of our life together! First, we realized how far down on our list of priorities our relationship had gradually slipped. Of course, we still loved each other and knew we would always stay married to one another. We got along well and talked a lot. However, our conversations had become focused on kids, job, finances, and all the other "stuff" that had filled our life. There was no longer much time to talk about US. It also dawned on us that we had slipped into some behavior patterns that created an even greater distance between us, like taking each other for granted, or functioning on our own separate agendas. We wanted to regain the sense of specialness that had filled us with joy in our early-married years. The icing on the cake was that we learned some communication tools on this weekend that we could take home and use to keep our relationship a daily priority. I could not fully explain the experience of the entire weekend in this small book, especially since the experience is unique for each couple who experiences it. However, I can tell you that we did go home and begin to take a small amount of time each day away from all the everyday distractions just to focus on each other. It is amazing what a difference only a few minutes a day can accomplish in keeping a relationship fresh!

Finding those few minutes each day can present a tremendous challenge in a busy household. Like any habit, it takes determination and persistence. Even small children can be taught to respect this established time, especially if they are included as important participants in the effort and given the opportunity to help. The ten to twenty minutes that we're trying to set aside is short enough for a child to endure, and it's an even more valuable experience if the child, or children, are rewarded with a few minutes of their own special time with their parents. This can become a habit that benefits the entire family.

This new routine developed in us an ability not only to communicate better with each other, but also with our kids and other people with whom we interacted. My personality tends to be that of one who will avoid expressing what is really on my mind if I judge that it might cause conflict. I was learning that I could communicate more openly in a non-offensive way that people actually appreciated. I could share with Bob negative feelings instead of holding them in and allowing them to fester. Bob, in turn, would appreciate my honesty and my trust in him that allowed me to share the things I found difficult to share before. Of course, for the sake our relationship, the sharing had to be without blaming. Blaming can be a trap we fall into that can drive a wedge between us. Thinking about our sharing as a gift for each other helps to keep the sharing positive.

I remember when I was feeling the frustration of seeing my neighbor's husband consistently come home at a reasonable hour every day, with an overnight duty rotation much less frequent than my husband's. Bob was working ten to twelve hours a day on his ship, in hectic preparation for a deployment, unlike our neighbor's ship, a tender, which usually remained tied up to the pier. As I repeatedly watched our neighbors enjoying frequent activities as a complete family, while the demands of Bob's job allowed him minimal time with us, resentment and bitterness began to grow inside me. At first, I was reluctant to share this with Bob because I knew that the immediate situation was beyond his control, and I judged that sharing these feelings with him would place an extra burden on him. Nevertheless, the longer I stifled the feelings, the more distant I became from him. I decided that for the sake of our relationship, I should risk sharing the negative feelings with Bob. When I did this, I was surprised at his positive response.

He had sensed that something was bothering me, and was relieved to find out what it was. He also expressed an appreciation for the trust I had in him to share negative things with him. We did not really solve the problem, but we now seemed more united in dealing with it together as best we could. I began to learn from that experience how freeing this kind of openness can be. This is an especially significant lesson for people pleasers like me who shy away from "rocking the boat." When we bring this sense of freedom to our relationships, the communication within the relationships becomes freer and more open. An upward spiral is created!

CHAPTER THREE

Strengthening

As the time approached when Bob's ship would go to sea, we began to consider how we might maintain Bob's presence with our young children during the separation. Since very early in their lives, he had read to them before bedtime. It is hard to know whether he or the children treasured that more. So, for weeks before the impending deployment, he recorded stories that we could play before bedtime while he was away. After Bob left with the ship, the kids really seemed to relish those few minutes each evening when their dad was away, listening to him read to them as they were accustomed. It wasn't quite the same as when they could snuggle up to him, but he certainly had a real, comforting presence to them, and to me, during those special story times. He was also very faithful in writing them little individual notes, letting each of them know that he loved them, and telling them little bits about what he was doing and places he was seeing. When he could purchase postcards, he would send one to each of us back home. We put up a map of the region where his ship was traveling, so we could follow his journey. It became a fun geography lesson. Mostly, it kept Bob "real" to us.

Another great opportunity came later in Bob's career, when our boys were older and able to participate in the Navy's traditional "Tiger Cruises." They were able to join the ship at some point during the ships' returns to homeport from long deployments. These are great special bonding times for sailors and their children, and I recommend that you make sure to take advantage of these opportunities if they become available to your family. The experience emphasizes how the quality of time that parents and children spend together can greatly compensate for the lack of quantity of time.

Spouses are not permitted on "Tiger Cruises," but sometimes there are opportunities to meet their sailors when a ship reaches a foreign port. This is what is known in the Navy community as "seagulling." The opportunity can be a bit of a pinch to the pocketbook, not to mention the difficulty in coordinating with the unpredictable ship schedules, which are always subject to change due to world events. Nevertheless, the experience can create shared memories for a lifetime. My once in a lifetime experience came when Bob's ship planned a ten day maintenance period in Israel. My parents came to stay with the children, and I flew to Israel (during a relatively peaceful time), where Bob met me at the airport. We rented a car, and were off on our adventure touring the Holy Land. What an amazing time we had, walking in ancient places where Christ and His ancestors before Him had walked! It put a bit of a burden on our budget, but we believe in the value of that time together, and the memories of it that we share today made it a worthwhile expenditure.

Our time in the Holy Land together was one way in which we were able to share and enrich the faith that has grown as an integral part of our relationship over the years. Sharing faith, no matter what that faith may be, can be a key factor in maintaining a close relationship during the course of a military career, whether that career lasts four or twenty-four years. It may start by simply finding the spiritual common ground in a marriage. Ideally, that takes place before the marriage. However, a couple can begin this process during their marriage and certainly experience the benefit of connecting on a spiritual level. It may begin simply with discussion between spouses about who God is to them and what role He plays in their lives. This sort of conversation may feel awkward to some at first, but it becomes more comfortable with practice. Another piece to this spiritual connection is shared prayer. It can be memorized prayers that can be prayed together, or it can be prayers that just come from the heart. The length of time spent in prayer is not as important as the consistency. A few minutes spent each day together in prayer will soon result in a wonderful bonding of hearts. This can even be done during separations by simply choosing the prayer and the time of day each partner will pray. It's a pretty powerful experience of connectedness!

There are many variations on the idea of shared daily prayer during deployments. Scripture offers a wonderful opportunity to share in the experience of God's word. Before a deployment, the couple can decide on where to begin and how much to read each day. This experience becomes much richer if the couple agrees to journal after each reading, thereby sharing with one another the personal message that each is hearing from God. To avoid making it too difficult to fit into busy schedules, it's a good idea to keep both the reading and writing times brief. The journaling can be done on loose-leaf paper, so that a week's worth of writing can be mailed at a time. If you have the benefit of internet technology at your disposal, the exchange can take place even more simply and more often. The experience of time spent with God each day is even richer when we do it with the knowledge that our spouse is also engaged in this endeavor. We experience a real sense of God's presence in our marriage! Many faith expressions offer little booklets of short reflections based on daily Scripture readings. Most are inexpensive enough to be purchased in duplicate, and are excellent material to read together and journal on across the miles. Some examples are: *Living Faith*, published by Creative Communications for the Parish, *The Upper Room*, published by Upper Room Publications, and *Living Each Day*, by Rabbi Abraham Twerski.

Information about subscribing to or purchasing these publications is located on pages 79–81.

Another variation of this shared journaling can be an addition or alternative to Scripture, meditation booklets, or prayer. We have found this variation very helpful in staying in touch with one another. Many couples write short daily accounts during deployments. What Bob and I learned to include in those accounts were our own reactions to what was going on in our lives. Adding our own thoughts and feelings about our daily experiences gave another dimension to simply keeping each other up to date about our lives away from each other. When Bob shared what was going inside him during his days of deployment, I had a stronger, more comforting sense of presence with him.

If these ideas sound strange or awkward to you, I advise you to try at least one of them anyway. Most skills that we acquire (like riding a bike) are awkward for us at first, but become more familiar, more comfortable, and more beneficial with time. These daily practices also require some persistence in developing long-term habits. Most habits become established when they are repeated without fail for twenty-one days. So, give yourself time. It helps to focus on the love you have for your spouse and your desire to have the best marriage possible. You can create together a sense of shared victory over the adversity of separation and of overcoming the hardship together. You will have a confidence that your relationship is stronger than ever.

Establishing ways to stay connected during deployments is more beneficial if done before the deployments. The time immediately preceding a deployment is usually very hectic, filled with preparations such as legal and financial affairs and car and home maintenance. This is all for the care and welfare of the family. What about the care of the relationship that is the core of the family? Dedicating time to decide how best to maintain a close couple and family relationship should be at the top of the "to do" list! Go on a date and put the hubbub on hold for a couple of hours to focus on each other. I read a story that has been circulating around the internet about an Army wife whose husband was deployed to the Middle East. Before his departure, they had gone on a date to a favorite restaurant, and they agreed that she would come to the restaurant on a certain day each month. This time would give her respite time from all the duties of maintaining their home, and would continue to be their special time of connection when they could both remember the special times they had shared. The story proceeded to tell of an incident when the wife was in the restaurant during her husband's deployment. During her meal, she overheard a loud discussion among a group of women at the next table generally criticizing the war in Iraq and ridiculing the military. After sitting quietly for a while, the Army wife finally arose, approached the women, and politely reminded them of the sacrifices the people of the military make to insure their freedom of speech. The women soon left, and other patrons showed appreciation for the wife's courage. What caught my attention was the couple's idea to continue having their "date" even during the separation. Although the husband could not be physically present during those times, he knew that she was there, spiritually and emotionally connected to him. His generosity in desiring this little treat for his wife further endeared him to her. It sounds like a good idea that I wish we had thought of when Bob was deployed. Of course, I enjoyed getting together with the other wives of Bob's shipmates, but that special one on one time to call to mind the presence of one's beloved sounds like a good way to foster intimacy during a deployment. Why not give it a try?

It's great if the deploying service member can make a date with each child as well. Identify an activity that would be special to the individual child, and that would provide an opportunity for interaction between the parent and the child. It need not be costly. A trip to the park, a bike ride, or going for an ice cream can be a special memory for both parent and child. Perhaps the parent and child can begin an ongoing project like planting a small garden or beginning a craft. The child can then feel a special connection with the parent during the separation, and can send progress reports that can help the parent continue to feel a bond with the child. The parent remaining at home will further foster couple intimacy by assisting the child to maintain good communication with the deployed parent.

Be sure to take time as a couple before deployment to choose together a daily routine during the deployment, utilizing whatever suggestions work for the two of you. Picking a certain time each day, keeping in mind the difference in time zones, is a way in which each spouse will know that the other is focusing on them at that moment, creating a powerful little moment of connectedness! This may be difficult for the service member who is out in the field or aboard ship, but if the service member has a watch with alarms, he or she can use the watch as a reminder of the spouse's particular thoughts and prayers at that moment.

CHAPTER FOUR

Savoring

There are a number of group programs that are effective in helping a couple boost their relationship before a deployment such as Marriage Encounter and other established marriage enrichments. There is a small group study program entitled, *Defending the Military Marriage*, which can be purchased in booklet form. It consists of four sharing sessions dealing with some very pertinent relationship issues. The benefit of addressing these issues in small group settings is that we hear a variety of insights that can help us process our own situations. In small groups, we increase our awareness that we're not alone or unique in what we're encountering, and we develop a support system in which we know others share our values. We learn that there are other couples who also want more than simply to survive a deployment. They also want to emerge as couples who have grown closer through the experience of separation. A small group sharing can create for us a confidence that this is possible. Knowing there are others nearby, in the midst of a deployment, who share the same values for their marriages, can be a valuable source of encouragement.

When couples are able to develop a stronger sense of unity during deployments, they often begin to experience enlightened moments of awareness of each other's presence. These can be awe-filled moments to revel in your couple connectedness. I was blessed with such a moment during Bob's only deployment that included the Christmas holidays. His ship was on a Mediterranean cruise, and pulled into Naples, Italy shortly before Christmas Day. A tour to Rome was arranged for those on the ship who were interested. The highlight of the tour was Midnight Mass at St. Peter's, with the Pope presiding and a couple thousand of his "closest friends" in attendance! Bob called to tell me this was going to take place. Wow! I thought that this was surely making lemonade out of lemons! I learned that the Mass would be rebroadcast in the U.S. at midnight local time. So, we stayed up, along with my in-laws, who had come to celebrate Christmas with the kids and me, and watched the beautiful ceremony on television, knowing that Bob was there among the throngs of people. We were aware that the event had taken place six hours before; but that did not diminish our sense of oneness with Bob. As far as we were concerned, we celebrated the birth of our Savior with him! Bob and the Infant Jesus were both unmistakably present to us!

We know other military couples who have strived for the same connectedness of which I have been writing throughout their years of service. I say, "their years of service," because I believe that what is given in service by a military person is certainly given by the military couple. Some of those couples have shared stories about their efforts to strengthen their own couple connectedness. I share them with you now, with hope that they will not only warm your heart, but also provide you with more ideas about fostering your own connectedness.

A thread that runs through each of these personal accounts is that these couples were actively nurturing their relationships long before being faced with separation. It's a lot easier to foster intimacy when you're apart if this is an ongoing quality in your relationship. This takes some effort by both partners. Many of our life's treasures need polishing up every now and then. The treasure of our marriage relationships thrives on regular attention. We receive what we put into them. Good relationships don't just happen! Your marriage will survive and be strengthened, as gold tested in fire, if you are already nurturing it!

I remember well the times of preparation, immediately preceding the deployments of Bob's ships. Those chaotic times required getting many different affairs in order. There's so little time to fit in all that needs doing. But I urge you to make your love affair a priority! Your marriage is meant to last long beyond active duty. So make some time to decide together what you will do to strengthen your connection. Each different idea is offered with the hope that one or two might work for you, or trigger a new idea of your own. I would love to hear about your ideas, and invite you to share them with me on my website, which you can find at the end of this book.

I also recommend that you go on a date before the separation. It need not be lengthy or costly, but it must be romantic! Your pleasure in each other's company will give you an extra joyful moment to hold onto and add to your treasury of memories. If babysitting is an issue, trade off children with another couple. The world we live in today does not generally seem to place much value on marriage, but I am here to tell you that you, as a married couple, are so very important to the future of our world! Our Creator established society based on the family unit, and He placed husband and wife at the core of that family. Don't shortchange your treasure. Please give it the time and attention it deserves! Not only will you benefit, but so will the world in which you live.

CHAPTER FIVE

Lyn's Story

"Hi Love, Hope you are remembering to deadhead the roses." This was the first line of an e-mail from my husband while he was at sea late one night last summer. The first thought that flashed through my mind was, "Oh it's a good thing that you are out to sea right now, or I'd be ready to 'deadhead' you!" It was 10:30 PM, I had just come in from watering the garden and I was beat. It had been a long day and I just wanted to check e-mail and head to bed. We have a mini-farm, 3½ acres, in Port Orchard Washington. We have four horses, three dogs and a cat that belong to us. Other animals that have learned that we have an open door policy drop by for a meal: A cat that has been living under our front porch for over a year now loudly reminds me when the cat feeder is empty, and a couple of dogs show up every morning for cookies in the barn. Ted, my husband, says it's because I have a big sign on my forehead that says, "sucker." I prefer to believe that animals know that I love them all and that I will be here to take care of them. As I sit here writing this, one of our black Labs, Bruno, is woofing at me to get his ball out from under the desk! Well maybe "sucker" is the right word!

God gave me a wonderful gift, a lively sense of humor. So, after a few minutes of fuming about Ted's reminding me to deadhead the roses, I started to laugh. It is so like Ted to think of little things like that in the quiet hours when he is out to sea. He loves to work in the yard, and it is hard on him when he doesn't get to see the fruits of his labor when his patrol schedule takes him away from home in the spring and summer. I love the results of his hard work too, even if I end up out in the yard until 10:30 at night watering the garden, the flowers and the 200+ trees that he has planted. Our home and yard is a haven of growth, and I believe it comes from the love we have for each other and all living things.

Being a military family has its ups and downs. One of the downs is, of course, the frequent moves. It is hard to put down roots when you move every couple of years. Some would say, "Why bother, you just have to tear them up all the time." We never have felt that way. We establish roots every time we move, and think about transplanting them instead of tearing them up with each move. Planting gardens, flowers and trees everywhere we go is just one way we put down roots. It makes things beautiful while we are there, and we leave them for the next family to enjoy. We leave a little part of us and transplant the rest. Our life has been one of love and growth for us, our children and for all the living things in our life. Therefore, deadheading the roses is just one way I can show my love for Ted and keep things growing while he is gone. I know that when he is home, he will help me muck stalls and care for the critters that share our life. We are partners in our life of love and growth, and our roots are strong and transplantable. God has truly blessed us, Ted with a very green thumb and me with Ted, someone with whom to share a life filled with living things.

Lyn Lindstrom is the wife of Coast Guard Captain Ted Lindstrom. They are a couple whose love for each other has spilled out not just to the plants and critters, but to the people they encounter wherever they move.

Lyn's story gives us a great example of how a couple can stay connected by sharing something they both love and in which they are both invested. You can adapt this idea to whatever interests you and your spouse share, whether it be gardening, sports, the arts, community service, or whatever you enjoy together. Something creative is probably better, because as you share about it, there can be a sense of mutual participation in cultivating something of value to the world, even when you're half a world apart. The key to making this model work for you is to develop such an interest together while you're still together. This gives the spouse who will be away a chance to "sow the seeds" of your shared interest, and then watch them "sprouting" from a distance with a sense of sharing in its origin. It's a little like having a baby together, although what I'm talking about is beyond the interest a couple shares in the family they have produced. Certainly, you will want to be sure to keep the deployed spouse up to date on the details of your children's lives. They are certainly a beautiful manifestation of couple love, and what parent doesn't feel invested in the children? However, a special interest aside from the children can foster an even stronger bond, an added sense of intimacy. These days, it's quite quick and easy to send photographs. In addition to sending pictures of the kids, you might find it fun to send pictures related to your shared special interest. If it's sports you enjoy together, try sending clippings from the sports page. Give your imagination free rein in tailoring a way of keeping the shared interests of your unique relationship alive and fresh even when you can't be together.

CHAPTER SIX

Chris' Story

My husband is a Marine of 22 years, and when we married I knew very little about being "in the Corps," as they say. My life since that time has been anything but dull. Many deployments and several children later, our relationship is stronger than ever, mostly due to our commitment to communication of our hearts. Our communication or "communication of our hearts" has evolved. It began as just sharing information of our daily life to sharing what's important to us in a more intimate way by sharing things that really are about our very personal love for each other, our marriage and commitment to each other. For example, I am a complainer (by self-proclamation) and in being a complainer, I complain a lot usually to the one that I love the most, (a.k.a. my husband). Early in our marriage he mentioned that in a few hours I had said, "I have a headache" about fifteen times. So he told me, "After three times of your saying anything, I am going to call you on it." He does this to this day by saying, "Oh you say you have a headache?" So now I try not to say things more than three times, sometimes even less. Instead, I communicate the important things that he may actually be able to help me with rather than continually complaining about my head-ache. The reason this is ok is because I know he HEARS me the first time I mention it.

This type of communication is espe-cially important when he is deployed. Our time is so limited when we talk: we want to share what is really important. An example of our communications of the heart is when talking on the phone when he is deployed we certainly say, "I love you." We used to spend most of the phone time with one or both of us rambling, "I love you so much and miss you so much and wish you were here." Now that we have grown in our love for each other, we, of course, still say we love each other and miss each other, but we quickly move on to, "This morning at 6 am when you would normally lean over and kiss me good morning, I missed you." So much more is said by that than by just rambling over and over again, "I miss you," because he and I both know that the morning kiss before leaving for work is a beautiful marriage tradition of ours, one that is truly missed when we are apart.

We've found that making the most of

the actual talking time we have when separated works well for us. For instance, the last deployment (Bahrain for six months last year), was exceptionally easier for "communication" because of email access. But it also seemed because of the nature of email . . . sometimes the important matters of the heart, spoken by the heart and heard by the heart best, are harder to read on an email. We found that saving some of the "special" stuff for phone calls made it something to cherish until we spoke to our spouse to share directly with them. I actually wrote a list by the phone of special things that happened that I wanted to share with him, when and if he was able to call. The last deployment proved to be a little easier for him to call, but rather than waiting by the phone, we planned that he try to call once a week (or every two weeks if he was out in the field) on a certain day and near a certain time. So that way we were not waiting by the phone or missing his call and feeling guilty. We looked forward to it, and were able to face the week a little brighter knowing he would try to call then. Of course, with the inconsistency of phone service, we still had to understand when that call was not able to get through to us. That is not always as easy as it sounds for the children or for the grown-ups!

We also made a habit of actually writing letters (by snail mail) and truly sharing those intimate parts of ourselves: sadness (without our spouse home to warm us at night and the simple comfort knowing they are near), or excitement (of their impending return), loneliness (without our partner to lean on throughout the hectic days with children), or happiness (with something incredible that had happened recently, either with a child's progression or life's little gifts that find their way to you, despite your exhaustion.) And, while it was VERY important for us to discuss the matters of real life, plumbing problems (and what to do and whom to call) & children's misbehavior & aggravation with the commander for keeping my spouse away for so long . . . the spouse that is away can only hear that stuff once. Then every other time you say it, they can do no more than they did the first time you told them. So, rather than spending that precious heart to heart time spilling all the problems out. . . . we tried to state them, look for support, love and understanding from each other and then move on. This is a habit I am still working on, even as my husband plans to retire this summer!

Without a doubt, I am the most

blessed woman in the world . . . with a husband who is as committed to our children and me as he is to the Corps and our God. I feel so fortunate to have learned to communicate—in some ways, because of the separations.

Chris Coughenour Taraschke is the wife of Master Sgt. John A. Taraschke, presently stationed at Marine Corps Base, Hawaii, and a recent recipient of a Bronze Star for his service during Operation Iraqi Freedom. Chris is a teacher by profession, and currently home schools her children.

I believe that some points Chris makes about sharing our feelings honestly with one's spouse are important to consider. First of all, we should do it, even though this may be something we are not accustomed to doing. When a couple faces separation due to military service, there are many facets of the situation that naturally bring forth very strong feelings. Our feelings are spontaneous reactions that happen inside of us in response to what's happening around us. Family separation alone is a topic loaded with a tangle of emotions. When we add to that already complicated equation the knowledge that the service member will be entering into harm's way, we are probably approaching some of the most profound of all human emotions. Facing them and sharing them may be very difficult. But exchanging feelings on this level has a welding effect on a relationship! Because they are a part of who we are, sharing them with our spouse can lead to greater intimacy. Whether the feelings are negative or positive, they can be a great gift to our spouse if done in a spirit of self-giving.

Chris makes the point that she has found that once the feelings are shared, it is time to move on. Sharing feelings can quickly become a negative influence in a relationship if we continue to dwell on the same feelings. This is one way in which we can "dump" our feelings on our spouse, and then it is no longer a gift. Another form of dumping is blaming the other for our feelings. This can also be destructive. It's important to share feelings with thought and care. What I found both personally and from the experience of others, is that sharing a negative feeling often diminishes it and makes it easier to handle. The spouse who is on the receiving end of the sharing should be a sensitive listener, resisting the temptation to prepare an answer during the sharing. Truly listening and accepting the feelings can be a gift as well.

Chris also wanted to pass on ideas from a Navy wife who was a former neighbor, and someone Chris admires greatly. Chris wrote, "She and her two children experienced their husband and dad being away many times. She made it a bit easier for him to be a part of their every day lives by writing specific things on a regular calendar each day, things that impacted their lives in simple ways (losing a tooth) and even more exciting (learning to ride a bike/or learning to walk). Then at the end of the month, she included that calendar page in a box they sent every month with home-baked goods and drawings and pictures. She also emailed quite a bit, each evening one good email explaining her day with the kids, and at the end of the week, she printed these off and mailed them to him. Keryn sent the emails to her husband at the end of the month because he mentioned that he read them once on the screen and wished he could remember everything she told him, and once they were deleted, they were deleted. Instead she thought, 'I'll send them to him as a sort of book of our time while he was away.' It made him feel involved in and part of that memory that had taken place while he was so far away. It was a nice way of keeping in touch and reminding him of how important he was in their daily lives. He loved it!" Please use these ideas if they appeal to you.

CHAPTER SEVEN

Jaye's Story: Being Rich

We prowled through the second hand bookstore, the day after Christmas, just my husband, Louie, our daughters, Jenny and Helen, and me. This was a precious time for us, because we would be splitting up as a family, again, in just a couple of days.

It had been a tough eight months since my husband had retired from the Navy. As plotters and planners, we had manipulated the "military system," while on active duty, as much as we could, trying to prevent a long, dreaded absence from one another. Now, here we were, retired, and we were eight months into our longest separation.

When my husband retired, we discovered that the only job available for him was in the city of Norfolk, Virginia. Our dream was to live out the rest of our lives in the mountains of southwestern Virginia, six and a half hours away. My health had gotten so bad, that it was impossible for me to stay with Louie in the city. We had settled for a separation, praying that a job would become available in the beautiful region that we love.

So, there we were, delaying the inevitable, passing time in a second hand bookstore, before the girls and I headed back to southwest Virginia. We were as broke as we'd ever been, supporting two households; yet we were grateful to be together, and we seized every opportunity for extra hugs, shared daydreams and laughter.

There was only one other person in the bookstore, besides the proprietor, a lovely, well-dressed, woman, about my age. I noticed her clothes, her shoes, and her expensive handbag, and I wondered what it would be like, to be rich enough to walk into a bookstore and have the money to buy any book my heart desired. But we were having so much fun, that I quickly forgot the woman.

We joked as we continued our treasure hunt, clutching our spending money of five dollars apiece, all hoping to be the first to find the oldest, least expensive book. It was a bittersweet excursion. Frequently, Louie and I would brush past one another, finding excuses to touch or to give one another's hand an extra squeeze.

Jenny remembered that there was an ATM machine not far from the bookstore, and she decided that she needed another twenty dollars that she had squirreled away. "No fair!" I cried, laughing. "The rest of us can only spend five dollars, and here you're going to have twenty-five dollars?!" We all laughed, and we began to tease Jenny, mercilessly, but she was able to convince her dad that she must have the $20, in order to get that irresistible book. "Come on, Jenny," Louie laughed. "I'll drive you to the ATM."

Then we did another round of hugging and kissing, none of us wanting to be apart for even a few minutes. Soon Louie and I would be saying "good-bye." We couldn't resist the opportunity to assure one another of our love, and our faith that our separation would soon come to an end. It must have been a curious ballet, this demonstrative family scene, but we were oblivious to what others might think.

Military families seem to fall into two categories: those who look for affectionate opportunities, and those who avoid close contact, because "good-byes" are painful. I have to admit that we're a pretty "huggy-kissy" family, so unmindful of anyone else, we continued to give kisses and hugs all around. In our military career, we had become painfully aware, that anything could happen during even the briefest separation. But now, as I look back, I realize how odd we must have looked.

Finally, in between another hug and kiss, I saw the perfect book for me! It was one hundred years old, and it was on my favorite time period, the Middle Ages. Oh, how I wanted that book! I quickly checked the inside cover for the price, and my heart fell. It was twenty-five dollars! We just didn't have it. I looked up at Louie, already knowing the answer.

He must have wanted me to have that book. I could see the pain in his eyes. Louie reached out and gave me an extra hug. I understood his "honey, we just can't afford it" message. I leaned into his sheltering arms, and I saw that the well-dressed lady was also touching the book that I wanted. Ah well, let her have it. I gave Louie an extra hug, and half-serious, I murmured, as my eyes locked with hers, "Oooohh, I wish I were rich!" "It looks to me, as though you already are." She said, with a smile.

There was a pause that stretched through eternity, and my heart filled with comprehension. I looked up at my husband, and I gazed at my daughters, wrapped as we were in the arms of love, and I knew it. I was rich. Very rich. I quickly turned to thank the woman for her gentle reminder, but she was gone!

Who was she? I'll never know. But

what she did for my outlook was nothing short of miraculous. I will never forget her. To where did she disappear? I can't say.

Strangely enough, within days, my husband received a job offer in south-western Virginia. In less than two weeks, he was hired and we moved to the place that is now our home. The job notice had been sent out two days before Christmas, even as we hugged and kissed and wished in that bookstore. Even as I heard the words, "It looks to me, as though you already are," events were already in motion to unite our family.

I am quite certain that it was all part of God's plan, to remind me of what being "rich" is all about: faith, love, family, and friends. And when I get to heaven, I will not be at all surprised to discover that God sent an angel to a second hand bookstore, in Norfolk, Virginia, to give me his richest message, the day after Christmas, many years ago.

Jaye Lewis is a writer and poet, who lives with her family in the Appalachian Mountains of southwestern Virginia. This story will be included in Jaye's forthcoming book, entitled *Entertaining Angels.* Jaye can be emailed at *jlewis@smyth.net*

Jaye's story reminds me of the wonderful abundance that comes to us as a result of simple gratitude. Each of us has something for which to be grateful. Simply waking up each day to a new day of life is a gift from the Creator, and starting each day in thankfulness is a great way to start the day. Not only do we have this gift of life, but also we have a special mate to share it with! When I think of all the lonely people in the world, or the people struggling to stay alive, I am definitely challenged to keep an attitude of gratitude!

Making gratitude a part of our daily life may require focused effort until it becomes a habit. Setting aside a specific few minutes the same time every day will help. Expressing gratitude to a spouse conveys that he or she is appreciated and not taken for granted. Showing appreciation for the everyday things your spouse does for you can be life giving. A simple "thank you" will trigger the desire to be even more giving. If we are grateful to our spouse, we need to tell them! This past Valentine's Day, I read in the newspaper a touching letter from a military man stationed on a remote tour of duty. In his letter, he told his wife how much he appreciated all she did to support him in his mission and to keep their family together despite all the hardships. It was a beautifully written message from the heart. No doubt, that expression of thanks was the most precious of treasures to his wife. Perhaps a plan to share with each other on a regular basis something about your spouse that you are thankful for could be included in your regular communication, whether you're together or apart.

CHAPTER EIGHT

Bob's Story

I have worked very closely with many married people during 25 years of active duty and dozens of deployments, from a few weeks to a year in length. I have seen how keeping a relationship connected, or not, influences the service member and the deployed unit.

I recall two incidents while assigned to a ship in 1989–1990. I reported aboard as a department head during a deployment to the Mediterranean Sea, and was encouraged to find that my senior division officer and principal assistant was an experienced Limited Duty Officer who had been aboard for two years. He was a superb technical expert who excelled at transferring his expertise to his technicians, who were responsible for the maintenance of all the electronics and communications equipment onboard. As the deployment proceeded, we became a team, and also close friends. Midway through the deployment, he started to lose focus, spending more time in his stateroom instead of being out with his sailors as had been his practice. When I talked with him about the change, he said that he had received a letter from home that had him a little upset, and that he would be better in a few days when we arrived in port and he could make a phone call. Well, things didn't improve after the port visit, and it wasn't long before he submitted a request for emergency leave to take care of critical family matters at home. He went home in the middle of the deployment, and then requested and received a humanitarian reassignment to shore duty near home because he had become, in effect, an instant single parent. His wife had decided, while he was gone, that she didn't want to remain in their 15-year marriage. We successfully completed our deployment, but losing an experienced leader made it more difficult than it should have been.

I was scheduled to transfer to shore duty in November 1990, and was preparing for an exercise above the Arctic Circle in August when Saddam Hussein invaded Kuwait. Less than a week later, we were loaded with Marines, their equipment, and several senior officers and their staffs, and were on the way to the Middle East. Throughout August and September, we conducted operations in the North Arabian Sea, outside the Persian Gulf, while preparing for the beginning of Operation Desert Storm. One night in late September, I was awakened and asked to go to the chaplain's stateroom. I began to think about which of the people in my department was going to receive a message from the Red Cross that required both of us present. When I got there, the chaplain gave me the message that Janel's dad had passed away. Luckily, the ship had a Military Affiliate Radio Service (MARS) radio station onboard, and by communicating with a volunteer radio operator in the states, who patched the signal through to a telephone, I was able to talk with Janel for a few minutes. She told me of her plans to take our kids to New Orleans for the funeral, and gave me their travel schedule. I looked at all the options for getting home in time for the funeral, but due to our location, the earliest I could arrive would be after Janel returned to Norfolk. Then it would be several weeks trying to get back, which would be more difficult because of all the people moving toward the area. Janel and I spoke again by MARS link and decided that it was better if I remained with the ship until I could come home after being relieved in six weeks. I felt closer to her during that time than I had in the weeks before. Our decision, based in communication and understanding, was not easy, but we still believe it was correct.

These two experiences are just examples of similar incidents I have witnessed many times. I have seen people perform flawlessly under conditions of significant stress when they knew they had the full support and understanding of their spouse, and I have seen others who were unable to concentrate on their duties because of concerns about their relationship with their spouse at home. Aboard ship, we literally live at work, so it is impossible to separate the personal from the professional aspects of our lives.

A military couple is a prime example of the interconnectedness of humanity, and how we can have an impact on people we don't even know. Being married to an active duty military person brings many challenges to us, many of which we would be happy not to face. But we face them as best we can because we will do whatever it takes to support our spouses toward the success of their mission and their military career. We may not wear the uniform, but we do fill an important role for the benefit of our country. It involves making the decision to love under often very trying circumstances. We have to keep in mind that how we decide to love and be present to our spouses makes a huge difference in our own lives, and also in many other lives.

Conclusion

Living the intimate life that God has called us to in marriage is a challenge for any married couple. For those who have been called to the service of our country, the challenge is multiplied! But to remain emotionally and spiritually connected is certainly possible with some extra planning and effort. Taking an idea from this book and making it happen may not be easy. If you have not done anything like this before, you may not be inclined to trying it. But I urge you to do it anyway. If your spouse is more eager than you are, trust him or her and decide to put your best effort into whatever you agree to do together. I can tell you that it will be well worth the effort to you. To grow, we must stretch, so I encourage you to stretch and try something new that can help you to grow closer to one another.

Maintaining a deep and personal level of communication will prepare you for an easier transition when you are reunited. Because of this, you will be well practiced in the communication needed to readjust to the life that you both look forward to enjoying when you are together again. You are much more likely to be on the same page, which will help you avoid some of the miscues that can occur when you have become out of touch with one another. Surviving a difficult time like separation with a sense of togetherness can be a bonding force like gold being tested in fire. The testing of your treasure can make your marriage stronger than ever. Despite the demands that accompany military service, your marriage deserves to be treasured by both of you at all times, with the awareness that the two of you together are always God's treasure. Strong marriages not only make a difference to couples and their families, but the whole world!

My goal for you, my purpose in writing this little book, is that you will come through military separation with a stronger marriage than ever! God bless you.

We would love to hear from you. If you would like to share your own story about how you have nurtured your marriage relationship during military separation, and/or read the testimonies of others, please visit us at *www.stayingconnected.net*, or write

Serviam Publishing/Staying Connected
P. O. Box 3467
Kingsport, TN 37664-0467

Resources
for Staying Connected

Daily Word for Couples, by Colleen Zuck, Janie Wright, and Elaine Meyer, is a 368 page paperback book filled with meditations, prayers, and touching true stories to help couples overcome obstacles, face new challenges, and rekindle the flame that first brought them together. It can be purchased online for $12.95 at *www.penguinputnam.com*

Living Each Day, by Rabbi Abraham Twerski, is a 406 page book available in both hard and soft cover. It provides an inspirational message and appropriate prayer for each day of the year, with Scripture. It follows the Jewish calendar. Christians may find the Old

Testament references inspiring, and
may enjoy exploring their faith roots.
This book can be found at *artsscroll.com*
or at *Amazon.com*. Prices vary.

Living Faith is a small paperback periodical published quarterly. It provides
daily reflection based on a Scripture
passage from the daily Mass. With
readings for daily Mass listed at the
bottom of each devotion, this booklet
helps Catholics pray and meditate in
spirit with the seasons of the Church
year. The short reflections are relat-
able to all faiths. To order, go to
www.livingfaith.com or write to Living
Faith Subscriptions, 1564 Fencorp
Dr., Fenton, MO 63026-2942. Pocket
size booklets cost $7.95 per year, with
discount rates for more than five
subscriptions. It is available in Spanish
and large print.

The Upper Room is another paperback booklet periodical published monthly. Each day's devotion offers a Bible verse, suggested Bible reading, reader-written meditation or story, prayer, prayer focus and thought for the day. To order, go to *www.upperroom.org* or write to The Upper Room, P.O. Box 37150, Boone, IA 50037-0150, or call 1-800-925-6847. A yearly subscription costs $9.00, with bulk rates available for more than ten copies. It is also available in Spanish and large print.

Defending the Military Marriage, by Lt. Col. Jim Fishback, USA (Ret.) and Bea Fishback, is an 80 page paperback book designed for use in four sessions of small group study to help military couples cope with—and even thrive—in their assignments. It is published by Family Life, 3900 North Rodney Parham Rd., Little Rock, AR 72212-2441. For ordering information, visit their website at *www.familylife.com* or call (501) 223-8663 or 1-800-FL-TODAY.

Worldwide Marriage Encounter is a weekend experience for any married couple who desires a richer fuller life together. The emphasis is on communication between husband and wife, who spend the weekend together away from the distractions and the tensions of everyday life, to concentrate on each other. The focus is on the interaction between husband and wife rather than group interaction. Please visit the very informative website at *http://www.wwme.org* or call 1-800-795-LOVE to find a weekend near you.

For a couple experiencing deep disillusionment in their marriage, a Retrouvaille weekend experience may be more helpful. Modeled somewhat on Marriage Encounter, it addresses how to heal the hurts that can destroy a relationship. There are follow-up sessions to continue the process that takes place on the weekend. This program has been very effective for couples who want to heal their relationships but are unsure how to begin. For more information, visit the Retrouvaille website at *http://www.retrouvaille.org* or call: 1-800-470-2230. Calls are confidential.

Share the treasure of
Staying Connected with others

Give the gift of loving relationship
to those you love.

Additional copies of *Staying Connected*
are available for $10.95,
plus $3.00 shipping and handling

Order today at
www.serviampublishing.com or by mailing:

Serviam Publishing
P.O. Box 3467
Kingsport, TN 37664-0467

Military Family Support Groups

Staying Connected is available at a
significant discount to use as a
fundraiser for your group.

Contact: *support@serviampublishing.com*
for more information